Written By: Anna DiGilio

All rights reserved. No part of this publication may be reproduced, distributed, or transmitted in any form or by any means, including photocopying, recording, or other electronic or mechanical methods, without the prior written permission of the publisher, except in the case of brief quotations embodied in critical reviews and certain other noncommercial uses permitted by copyright law.

For permission requests, write to the publisher:
Laprea Publishing
info@lapreapublishing.com

Website: www.GuidedReaders.com

ISBN: 978-1-63647-188-4

© 2020 Anna DiGilio

Photo Credits:
Cover, Title Page (top left), Cover, Title Page (top right), Cover, Title Page (bottom right), 3, 8 (top) 12 (top): Shutterstock; Andrey_Popov. Cover, Title Page (center): Shutterstock; Photographee.eu. Cover, Title Page (bottom left), 9: Shutterstock; New Africa. 4 (top), 10 (bottom): Shutterstock; Fizkes. 4 (bottom): Depositphotos; Vladacanon. 5 (top): Shutterstock; Mai Groves. 5 (bottom): Shutterstock; Allison C Bailey. 6: Depositphotos; Belchonock. 7: Wikimedia Commons/Ethnologue, Gallaudet, etc.; Kwamikagami at English Wikipedia. 8 (bottom): Depositphotos; Elnur_. 10 (top): Shutterstock; Juan Ci. 11: Depositphotos; Tiptoee. 12 (bottom): Shutterstock; Insta_photos. 13 (top, bottom): Depositphotos; Sckiw. 14 (top): Shutterstock; Littlekidmoment. 14 (bottom): Shutterstock; Watchara phochareung. 15 (top, bottom): Shutterstock; Adriaticfoto.

TABLE OF CONTENTS

What Is Sign Language?............................Page 4

How People Use Sign Language.............Page 8

Who Uses Sign Language?........................Page 9

Learning Sign Language............................Page 12

Glossary..Page 16

What Is Sign Language?

Some people talk with their mouth. Some people talk with their body. Sign <u>language</u> is talking with your body. Sign language is quiet. Sign language does not use the <u>voice</u>.

These people are using sign language.

Sign language uses hands. Sign language uses arms. Sign language uses faces. Sign language uses heads. People move many body parts to make signs.

Signs have meanings. Some signs are letters. Some signs are words. Some signs are ideas.

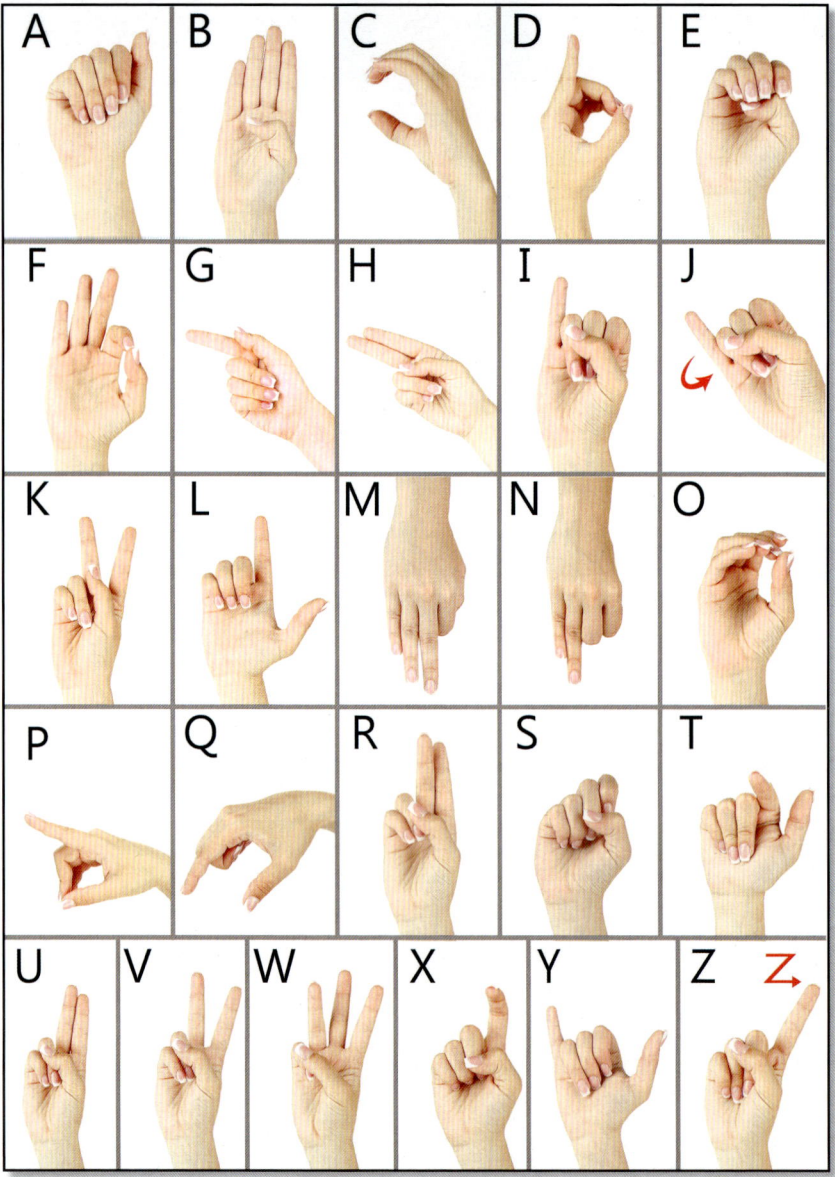

These signs are letters.

Many countries use American Sign Language. There are other sign languages, too.

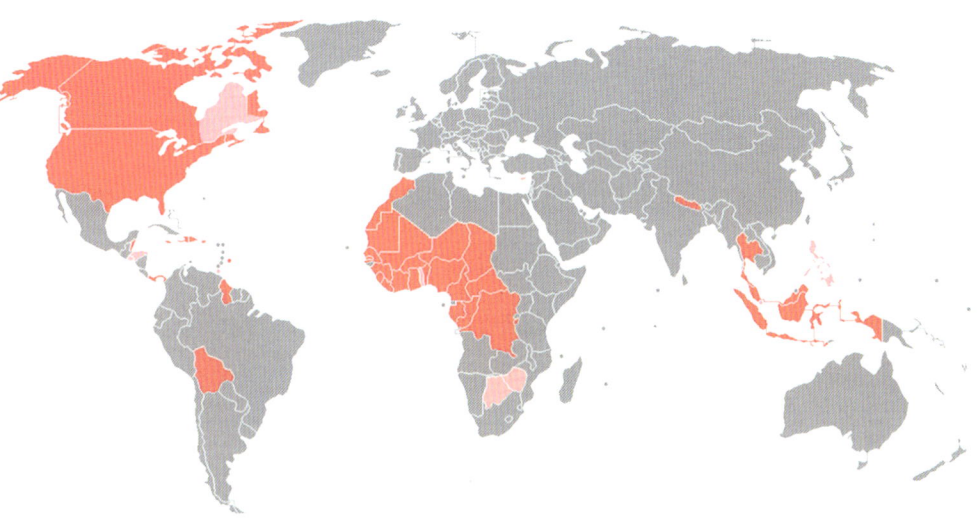

People in these countries use American Sign Language.
(Wikimedia Commons/Ethnologue, Gallaudet, etc.; Kwamikagami at English Wikipedia)

How People Use Sign Language

People use sign language for many things. They say hello. They ask questions. They say what they need. They say how they think and feel.

Who Uses Sign Language?

Some people cannot hear at all. These people are <u>deaf</u>. They use sign language.

Some people cannot hear well. These people are <u>hard of hearing</u>. They use sign language.

Some people cannot talk. These people are <u>mute</u>. They use sign language, too.

Some people are born deaf. Some people lose their hearing later. Sign language helps all these people.

How do people lose their hearing? Some people lose it when they get sick. Some people lose it when they get old. Some people lose it because of loud noises. Sign language helps all these people.

Loud sounds can hurt people's hearing.

Learning Sign Language

Many people use sign language. You can learn sign language, too. It's fun!

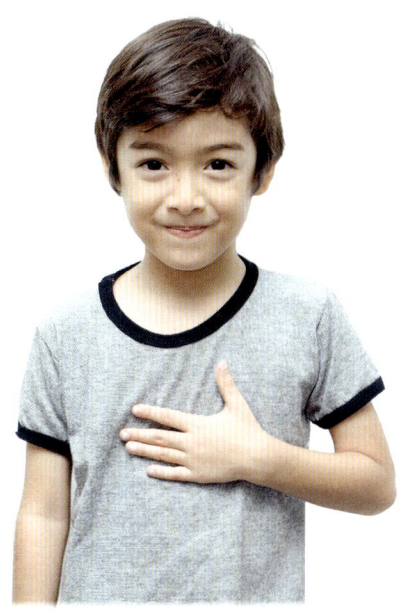

This sign means "please."

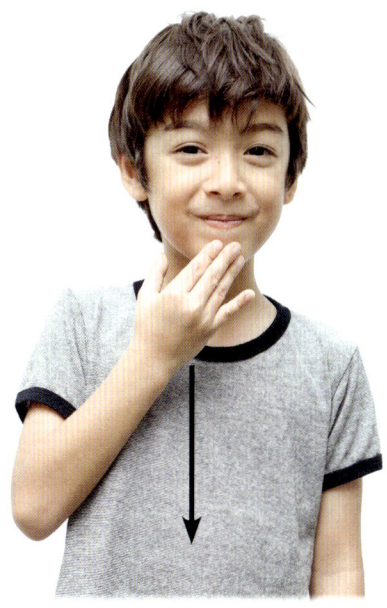

This sign means "thank you."

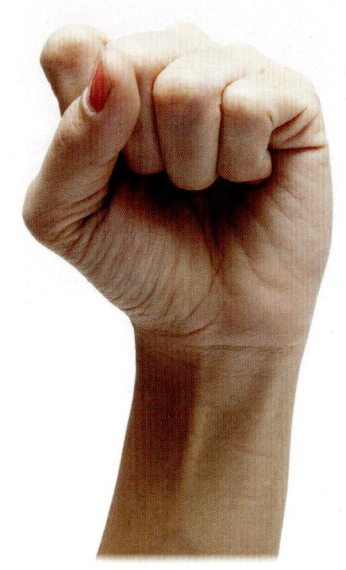
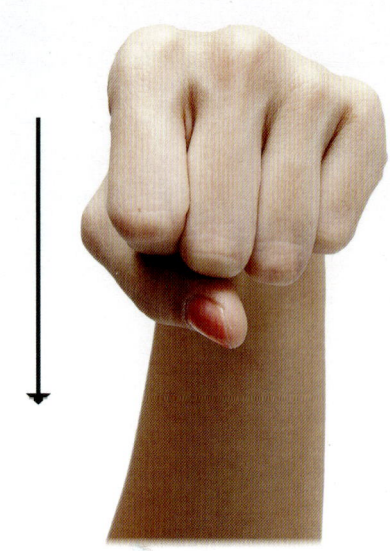

This sign means "yes."

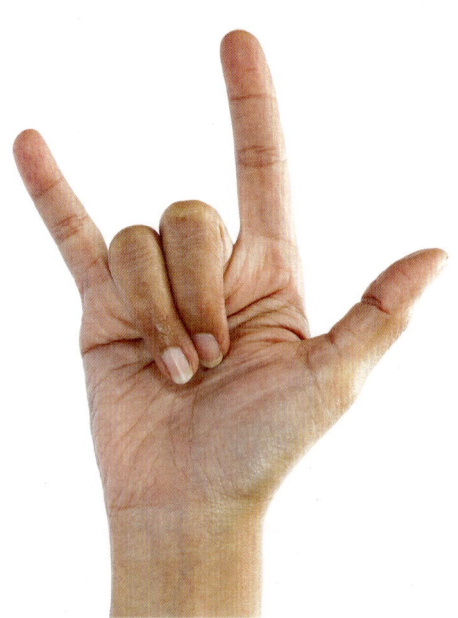

This sign means "I love you."

Underline: Practice sign language. You will get better and better!

GLOSSARY

<u>deaf</u>
not able to hear

<u>hard of hearing</u>
not able to hear well

<u>language</u>
a way to make thoughts and feelings known

<u>mute</u>
not able to use one's voice to speak

<u>practice</u>
to do something over and over to get better

<u>voice</u>
sounds made with the mouth and throat when speaking or singing